PIANO • VOCAL • GUITAR

THE BOOK OF GREATEST
Movie Music

D1535934

ISBN 0-7935-8806-5

HAL•LEONARD®
CORPORATION

7777 W. BLUEMOUND RD. P.O. BOX 13819 MILWAUKEE, WI 53213

Visit Hal Leonard Online at
www.halleonard.com

THE BOOK OF GREATEST
Movie Music

CONTENTS

BEAUTY AND THE BEAST
from Walt Disney's BEAUTY AND THE BEAST

Lyrics by HOWARD ASHMAN
Music by ALAN MENKEN

8

CAN YOU FEEL THE LOVE TONIGHT

from Walt Disney Pictures' THE LION KING

Music by ELTON JOHN
Lyrics by TIM RICE

CANDLE ON THE WATER

from Walt Disney's PETE'S DRAGON

Words and Music by AL KASHA
and JOEL HIRSCHHORN

I'll be your can - dle on the wa - ter,
I'll be your can - dle on the wa - ter,

My love for you will al - ways
'Til ev - 'ry wave is warm and

burn. I know you're lost and drift - ing,
bright, My soul is there be - side you,

But the clouds are lift - ing,
Let this can - dle guide you

don't give up you have some - where to turn.
soon you'll see a gold - en stream of light.

CHARIOTS OF FIRE

from CHARIOTS OF FIRE

Music by VANGELIS

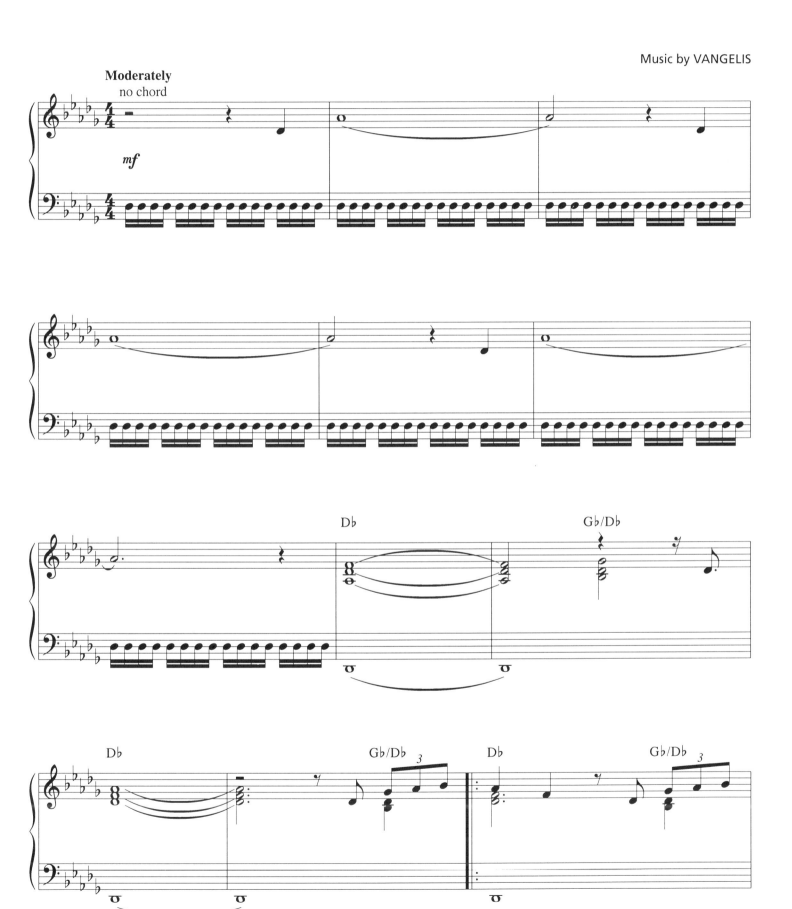

CHANGE THE WORLD
featured on the Motion Picture Soundtrack PHENOMENON

Words and Music by GORDON KENNEDY,
TOMMY SIMS and WAYNE KIRKPATRICK

CIRCLE OF LIFE
from Walt Disney Pictures' THE LION KING

Music by ELTON JOHN
Lyrics by TIM RICE

Moderately, with an African beat

Same tempo, gently rhythmic

(African chant continues)

through de - spair and hope,_____ through faith and __ love, 'til we find our place_____ on the path un - wind - ing ___ in the cir - cle,_____ the cir - cle __ of life.

8vb ---

COLE'S SONG

from MR. HOLLAND'S OPUS

Words by JULIAN LENNON and JUSTIN CLAYTON
Music by MICHAEL KAMEN

COLORS OF THE WIND

from Walt Disney's POCAHONTAS

Music by ALAN MENKEN
Lyrics by STEPHEN SCHWARTZ

A DREAM IS A WISH YOUR HEART MAKES

from Walt Disney's CINDERELLA

Words and Music by MACK DAVID,
AL HOFFMAN and JERRY LIVINGSTON

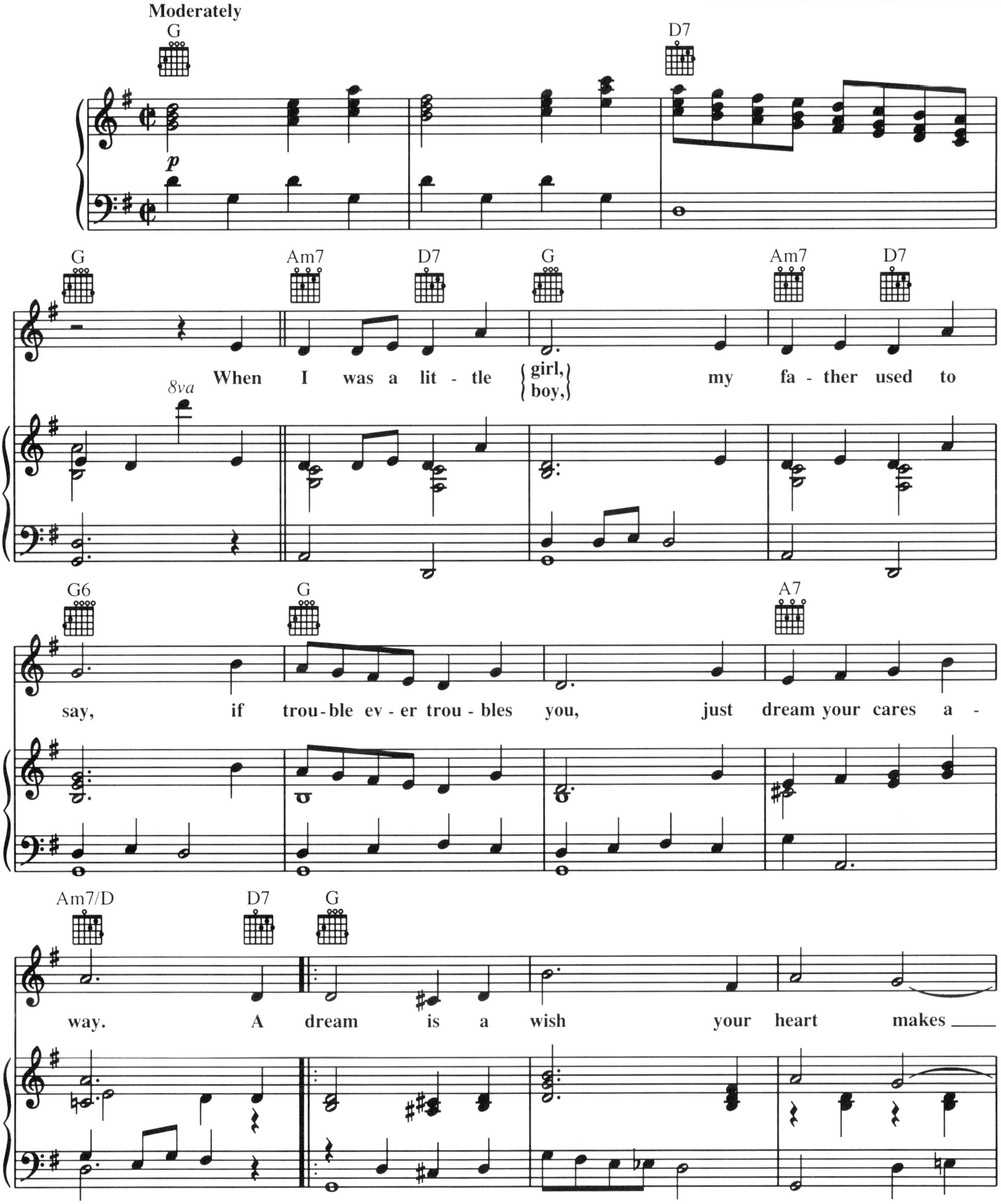

Lyrics:

When I was a lit-tle {girl, / boy,} my fa-ther used to say, if trou-ble ev-er trou-bles you, just dream your cares a-way. A dream is a wish your heart makes ___

47

COUNT ON ME

from the Original Soundtrack Album WAITING TO EXHALE

Words and Music by BABYFACE,
WHITNEY HOUSTON and MICHAEL HOUSTON

THE DREAME
from SENSE AND SENSIBILITY

By PATRICK DOYLE

I am un-done to-night. Love, in a sub-tle dreame dis-

guised, _____ hath both my heart and me _____ sur - prised, _

whom nev - er yet he durst at - tempt a - wake. _ Nor will he tell me for whose

sake he _ did me the de - light or

spight, _____ but leaves me to in - quire ____ in all my wild de - sire of

sleep a - gain, _____ who was his aid, and sleep so guil - tie

cresc.

and a-fraid, and since he dares not come ____ with - in

my sight. _____

THE ENGLISH PATIENT
from THE ENGLISH PATIENT

Written by GABRIEL YARED

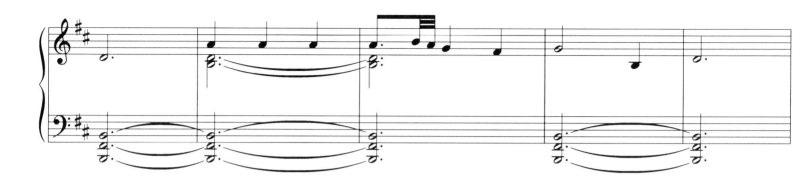

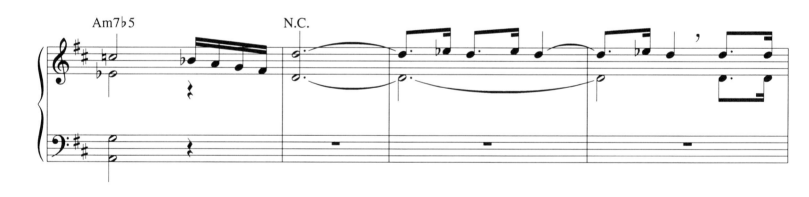

THEME FROM E.T.
(The Extra-Terrestrial)
from the Universal Picture E.T. (THE EXTRA-TERRESTRIAL)

Music by JOHN WILLIAMS

Piano Solo

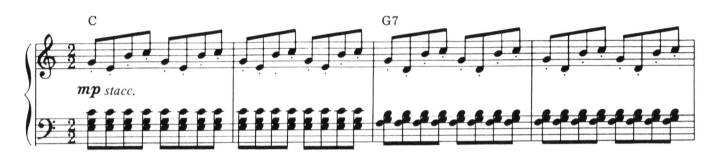

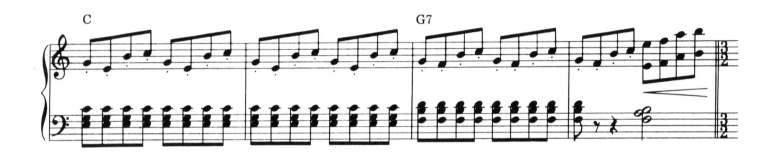

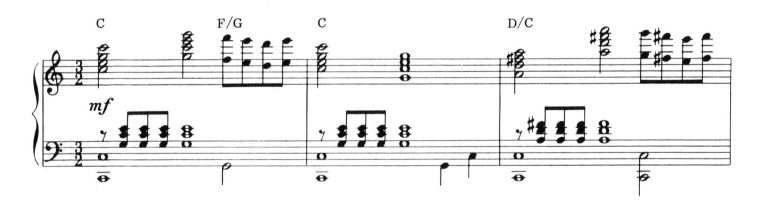

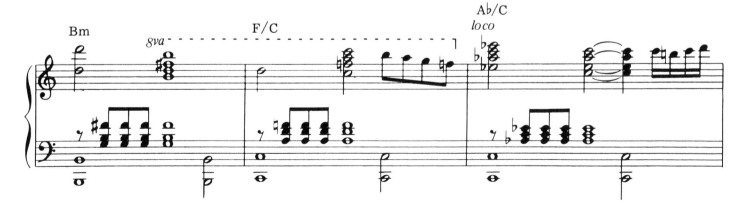

MCA music publishing

EXHALE
(SHOOP SHOOP)
from the Original Soundtrack Album WAITING TO EXHALE

Words and Music by
BABYFACE

FOR THE FIRST TIME

from ONE FINE DAY

Words and Music by ALLAN RICH,
JAMES NEWTON HOWARD and JUD FRIEDMAN

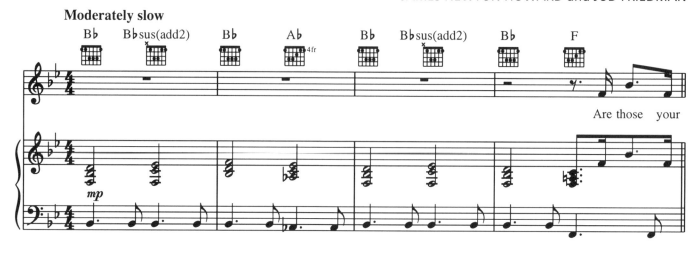

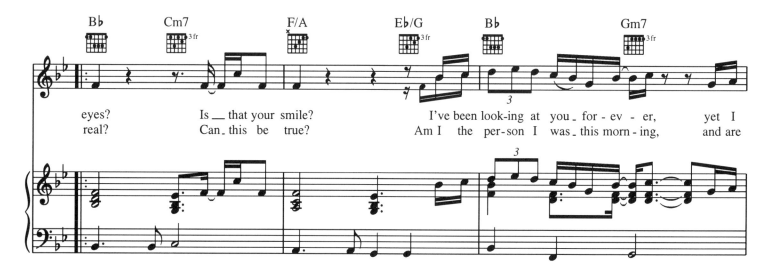

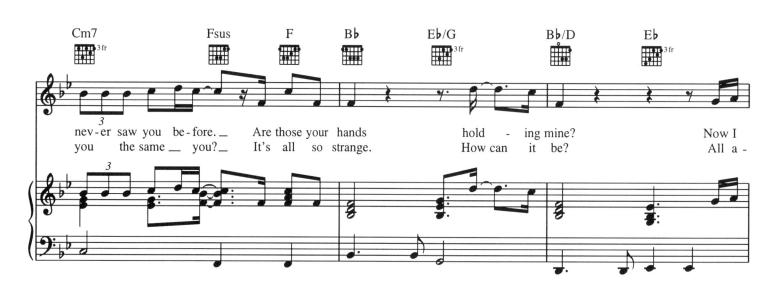

GALE'S THEME (MAIN TITLE)

from THE RIVER WILD

By JERRY GOLDSMITH

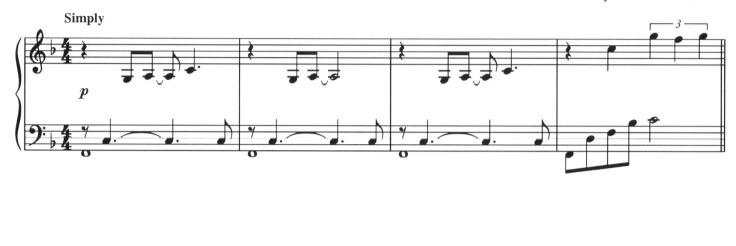

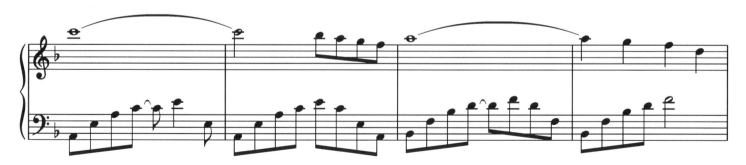

I FINALLY FOUND SOMEONE

from THE MIRROR HAS TWO FACES

Words and Music by BARBRA STREISAND, MARVIN HAMLISCH,
R. J. LANGE and BRYAN ADAMS

GOD HELP THE OUTCASTS

from Walt Disney's THE HUNCHBACK OF NOTRE DAME

Music by ALAN MENKEN
Lyrics by STEPHEN SCHWARTZ

I BELIEVE IN YOU AND ME

from the Touchstone Motion Picture THE PREACHER'S WIFE

Words and Music by DAVID WOLFERT
and SANDY LINZER

I SAY A LITTLE PRAYER

featured in the Tri-Star Motion Picture MY BEST FRIEND'S WEDDING

Lyric by HAL DAVID
Music by BURT BACHARACH

Lyrics (beneath staff):

(1.) The mo - ment I wake up,
(2.) I run ___ for the bus, dear.
(D.S.) *Instrumental solo*

be - fore ___ I put on my make - up, I
While rid - ing, I think of us, dear. I
(I

prayer. Say you love me, too.

Why don't you an-swer my prayer?

You know, ev-'ry day I say a lit-tle

Repeat and Fade

THEME FROM "THE LOST WORLD"
from the Universal Motion Picture THE LOST WORLD: JURASSIC PARK

Composed by JOHN WILLIAMS

Forcefully

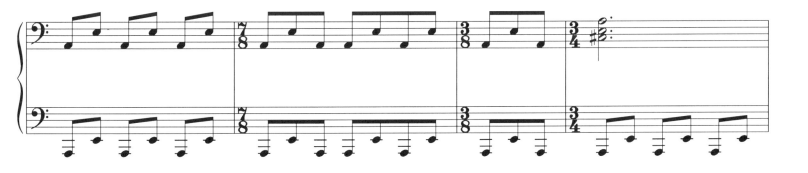

IL POSTINO
(The Postman)
from IL POSTINO

Music by LUIS BACALOV

Moderato

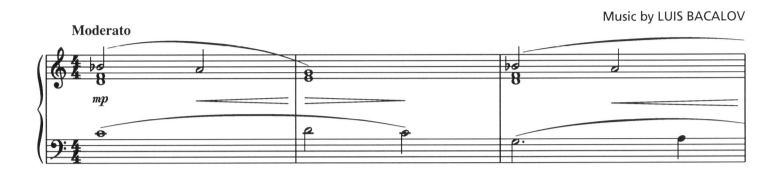

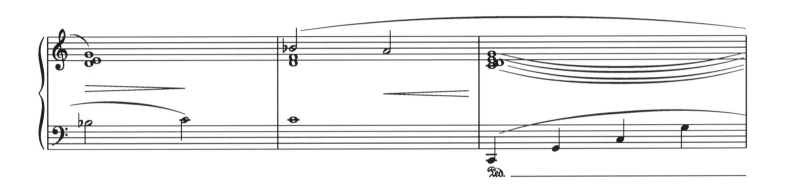

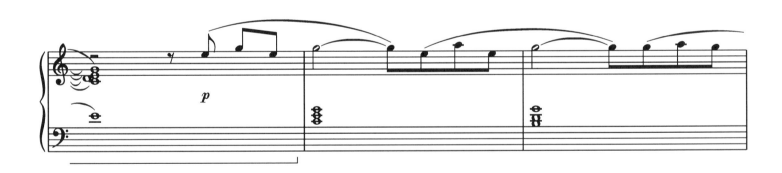

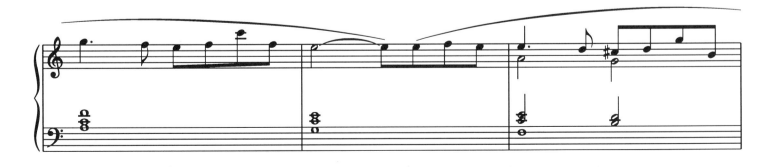

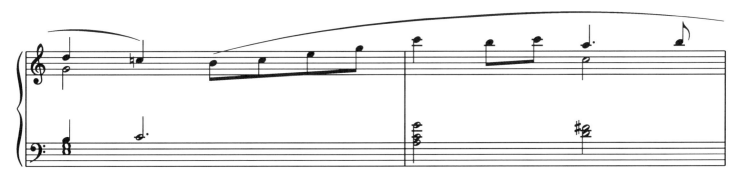

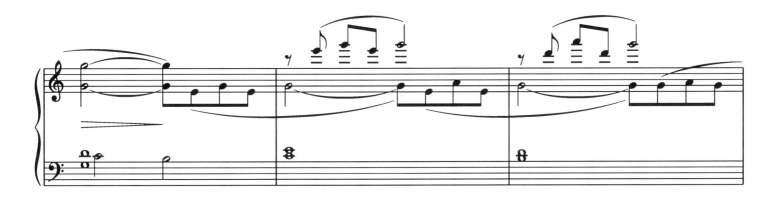

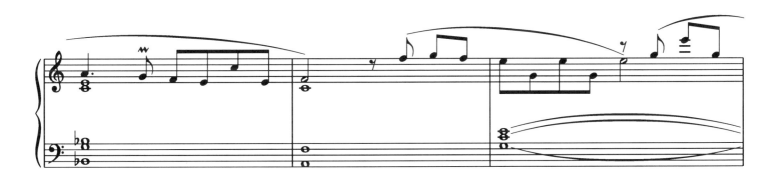

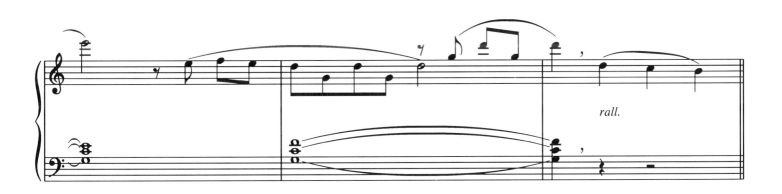

Mosso

A Tempo

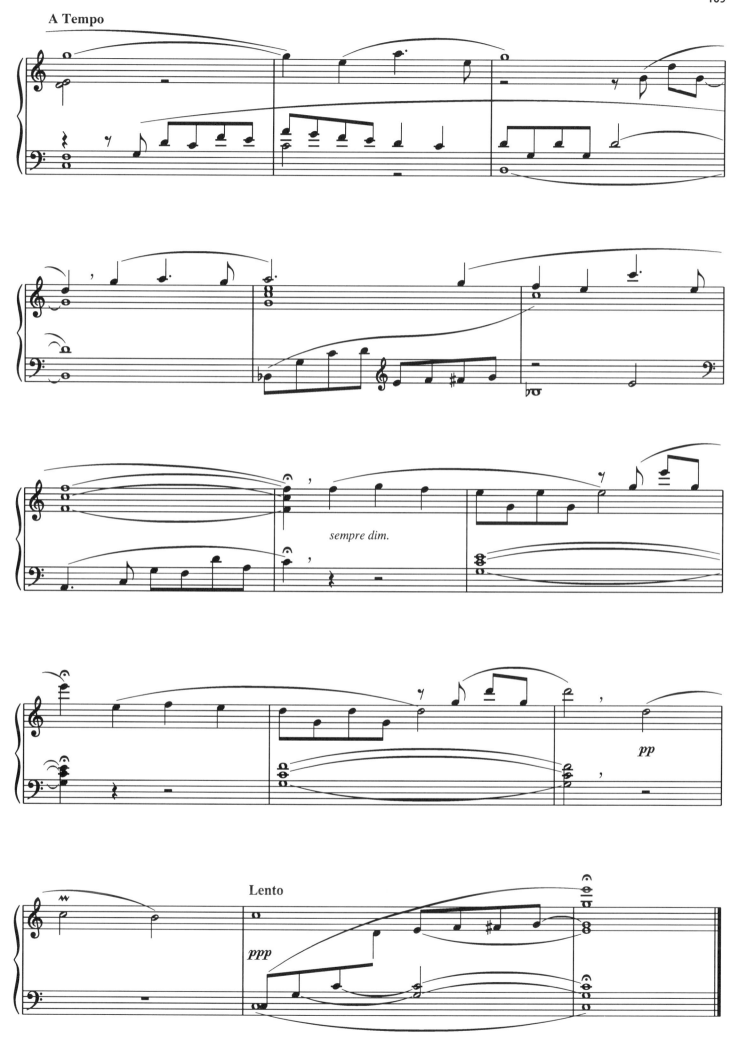

THE JOHN DUNBAR THEME
from DANCES WITH WOLVES

By JOHN BARRY

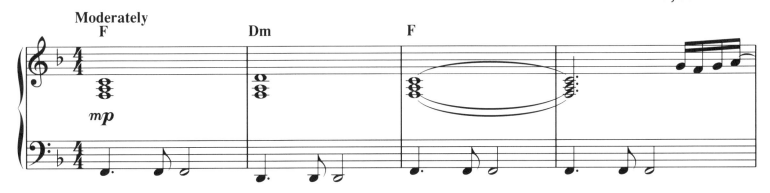

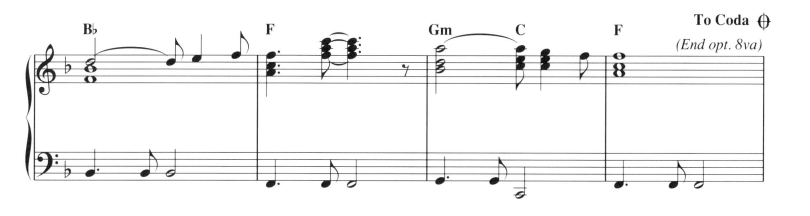

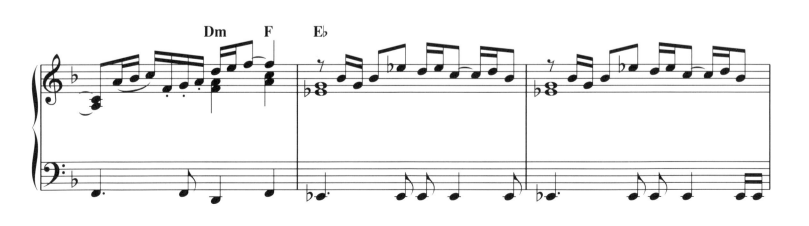

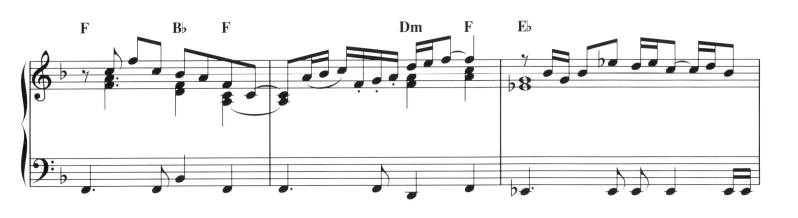

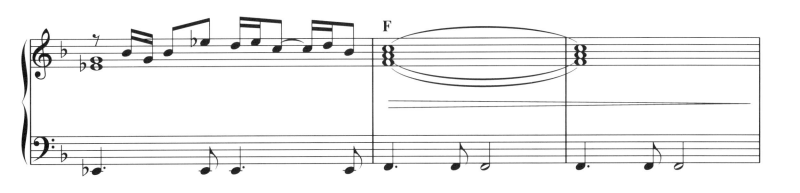

THEME FROM "JURASSIC PARK"

from the Universal Motion Picture JURASSIC PARK

Composed by JOHN WILLIAMS

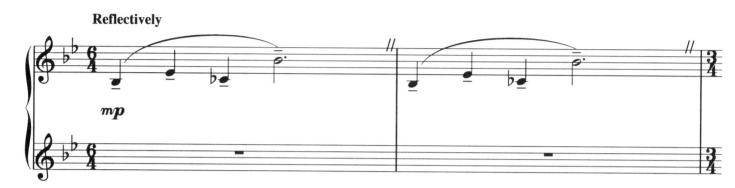

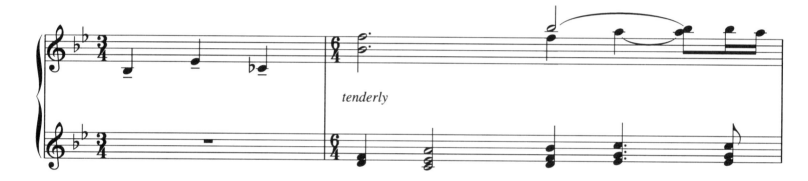

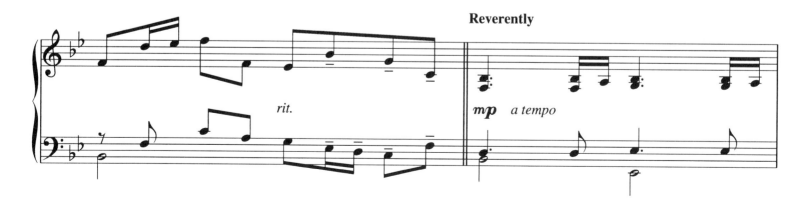

LOVE THEME
from CINEMA PARADISO

Music by ANDREA MORRICONE

Slowly, with motion

RIVER
from the Motion Picture THE MISSION

Music by ENNIO MORRICONE

Moderately

pp   *cresc. poco a poco*

Vi - ta, vi - ta no - stra tel - lus

p

no - stra vi - ta no - stra sic cla - mant. Vi - ta, vi - ta

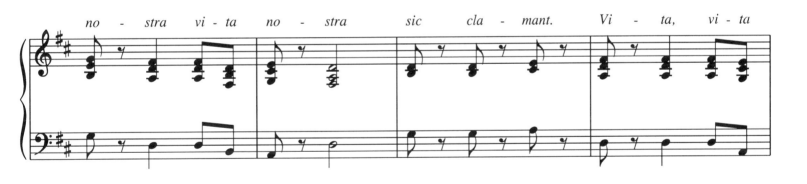

no - stra tel - lus no - stra vi - ta no - stra sic cla - mant.

MISSION: IMPOSSIBLE THEME

from the Paramount Motion Picture MISSION: IMPOSSIBLE

By LALO SCHIFRIN

126

To Coda

MOONLIGHT
from the Paramount Motion Picture SABRINA

Lyric by ALAN and MARILYN BERGMAN
Music by JOHN WILLIAMS

ONCE UPON A DREAM

from Walt Disney's SLEEPING BEAUTY

Words and Music by SAMMY FAIN and JACK LAWRENCE
Adapted from a Theme by TCHAIKOVSKY

I know you! I walked with you once up-on a

dream. _____ I know you! The

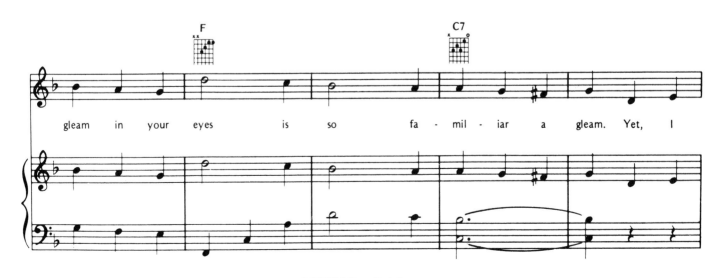

gleam in your eyes is so fa-mil-iar a gleam. Yet, I

REMEMBER ME THIS WAY

from the Universal Motion Picture CASPER

Music by DAVID FOSTER
Lyrics by LINDA THOMPSON

THEME FROM "SCHINDLER'S LIST"

from the Universal Motion Picture SCHINDLER'S LIST

Composed by JOHN WILLIAMS

SOMETHING TO TALK ABOUT
(Let's Give Them Something to Talk About)

Words and Music by
SHIRLEY EIKHARD

Moderate Reggae/Rock

Peo - ple are talk - ing, talk - ing a - bout peo - ple.
I feel so fool - ish. I nev - er no - ticed that,

I hear them whis - per, you won't be - lieve it.
ba - by, you're act - ing so nerv - ous, like you're fall - ing.

* Recorded a half step lower

A SPOONFUL OF SUGAR

from Walt Disney's MARY POPPINS

Words and Music by RICHARD M. SHERMAN
and ROBERT B. SHERMAN

In ev - 'ry job that must be done there is an
feath - er - ing his nest has ver - y

el - e - ment of fun; You find the fun and
lit - tle time to rest While gath - er - ing his

snap the job's a game; And ev - 'ry task you un - der -
bits of twine and twig. Though quite in - tent in his pur -

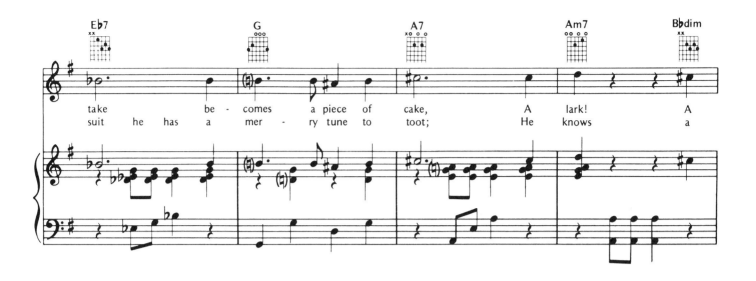

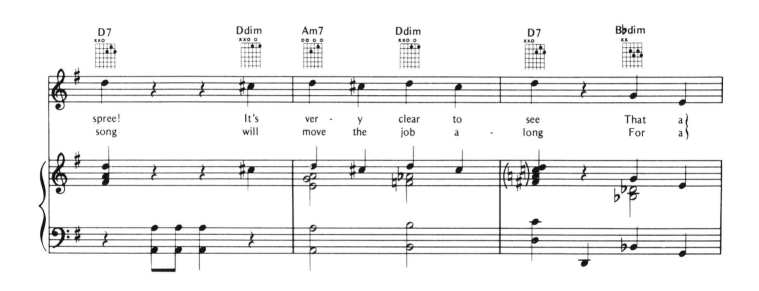

STAR TREK® - THE MOTION PICTURE
Theme from the Paramount Picture STAR TREK: THE MOTION PICTURE

Music by JERRY GOLDSMITH

TEARS IN HEAVEN
featured in the Motion Picture RUSH

Words and Music by ERIC CLAPTON
and WILL JENNINGS

Would you know my name _____
Would you hold my hand _____
Would you know my name _____

if I saw you in heav - en?
if I saw you in heav - en?
if I saw you in heav - en?

Would it be the same _____
Would you help me stand _____
Would you be the same _____

Be - yond   the   door ___   there's peace, I'm   sure.___

And I know___ there'll be no more___ tears in heav-

en.

THEME FROM
"TERMS OF ENDEARMENT"

from the Paramount Picture TERMS OF ENDEARMENT

By MICHAEL GORE

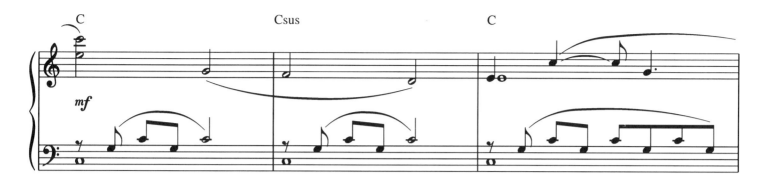

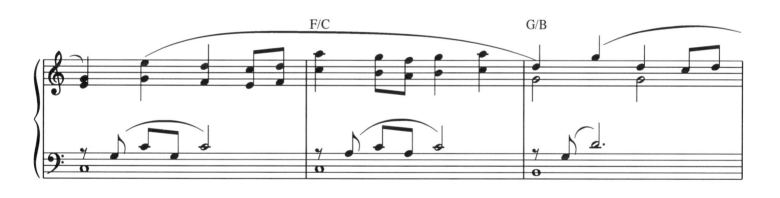

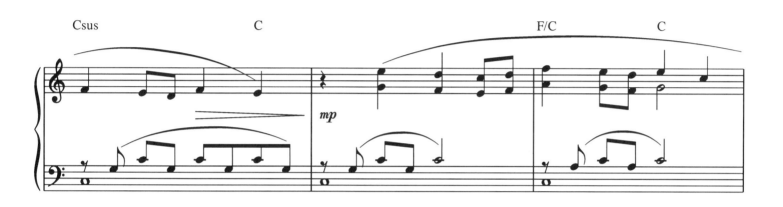

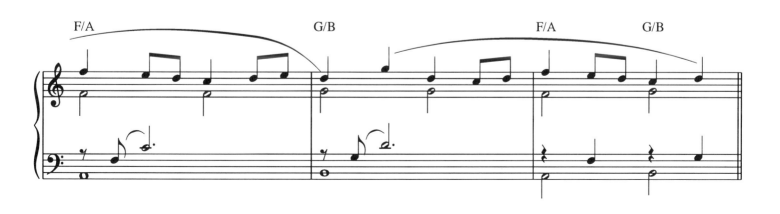

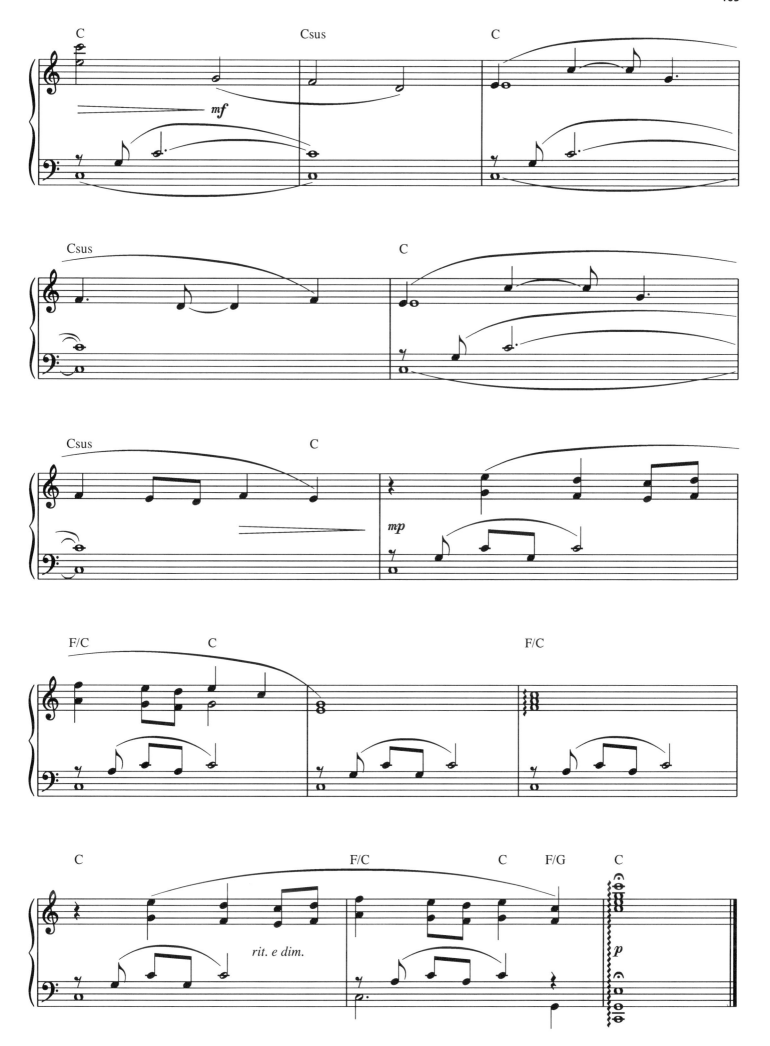

THAT THING YOU DO!

from the Original Motion Picture Soundtrack THAT THING YOU DO!

Words and Music by
ADAM SCHLESINGER

A TIME FOR US
(Love Theme)
from the Paramount Picture ROMEO AND JULIET

Words by LARRY KUSIK and EDDIE SNYDER
Music by NINO ROTA

Slowly and Expressively

A time for us some day there'll be when chains are torn by cour-age born of a love that's free. A time when dreams so long de-

THE WAY WE WERE

from the Motion Picture THE WAY WE WERE

Words by ALAN and MARILYN BERGMAN
Music by MARVIN HAMLISCH

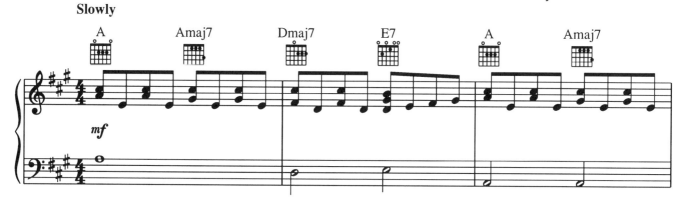

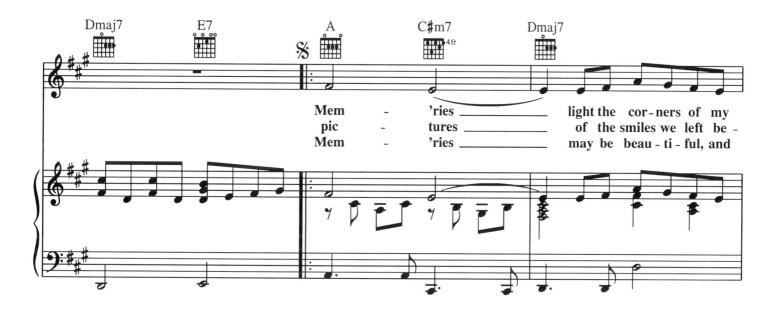

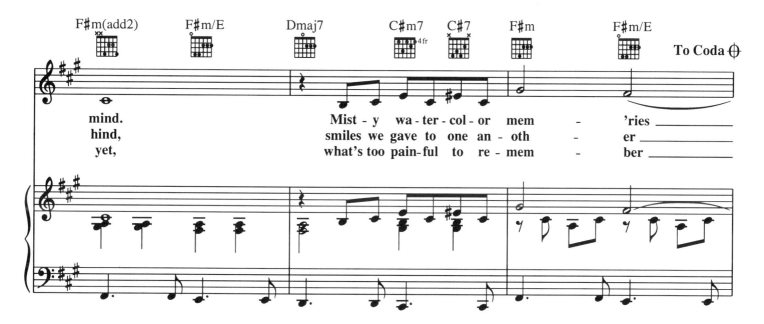

UNCHAINED MELODY
featured in the Motion Picture GHOST

Lyric by HY ZARET
Music by ALEX NORTH

178

Lone - ly riv - ers sigh,— "Wait for me, __ wait for me!"
All a - lone, I gaze — at the stars, __ at the stars,

I'll be com - ing home, — wait for me! _____
Dream - ing of my love __ far a - way. _____

As at first

Oh, my love, my dar - ling, I've hun-gered for your touch a

Tempo primo

long, lone - ly time. _____ Time goes by so

WHEN I FALL IN LOVE

featured in the TriStar Motion Picture SLEEPLESS IN SEATTLE

Words by EDWARD HEYMAN
Music by VICTOR YOUNG

A WHOLE NEW WORLD
(Aladdin's Theme)
from Walt Disney's ALADDIN

Music by ALAN MENKEN
Lyrics by TIM RICE

YOU MUST LOVE ME

from the Cinergi Motion Picture EVITA

Words by TIM RICE
Music by ANDREW LLOYD WEBBER

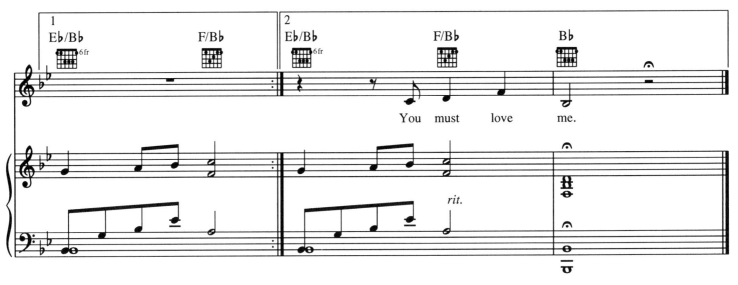

Additional Lyrics

Verse 2: *(Instrumental 8 bars)*
Why are you at my side?
How can I be any use to you now?
Give me a chance and I'll let you see how
Nothing has changed.
Deep in my heart I'm concealing
Things that I'm longing to say,
Scared to confess what I'm feeling
Frightened you'll slip away,
You must love me.

The Greatest Songs Ever Written

The Best Ever Collection
Arranged for Piano, Voice & Guitar

150 of the Most Beautiful Songs Ever
Over 400 pages of slow and sentimental ballads, including: Edelweiss • For All We Know • How Deep Is Your Love • I Have Dreamed • I'll Be Seeing You • If We Only Have Love • Songbird • Summertime • Unchained Melody • Young at Heart • many more.
00360735..$19.95

The Best Big Band Songs Ever
69 of the greatest big band songs ever, including: Basin Street Blues • Boogie Woogie Bugle Boy • Don't Get Around Much Anymore • In the Mood • Marie • Moonglow • Opus One • Satin Doll • Sentimental Journey • String of Pearls • Who's Sorry Now.
00359129..$16.95

The Best Broadway Songs Ever
Over 65 songs in all! Highlights include: All I Ask of You • Bess, You Is My Woman • Camelot • Climb Ev'ry Mountain • Comedy Tonight • Don't Cry for Me Argentina • Getting to Know You • I Dreamed a Dream • If I Were a Rich Man • Ol' Man River • and more!
00309155..$19.95

The Best Christmas Songs Ever
A collection of 72 of the most-loved songs of the season, including: Frosty the Snow Man • A Holly Jolly Christmas • Home for the Holidays • I'll Be Home for Christmas • Jingle-Bell Rock • Rudolph, The Red-Nosed Reindeer • Silver Bells • Toyland • more.
00359130..$18.95

The Best Classical Songs Ever
Over 80 of the best songs in classical music, including: Air on the G String • Ave Maria • Canon in D • Eine Kleine Nachtmusik • Für Elise • Lacrymosa • Ode to Joy • William Tell Overture • and many more.
00310674..$17.95

The Best Contemporary Christian Songs Ever
A great collection of 50 favorites by top artists. Includes: Awesome God • El Shaddai • Father's Eyes • Friends • God Is in Control • In the Name of the Lord • Jesus Freak • People Need the Lord • Place in This World • Serve the Lord • Thank You • Thy Word • more.
00310558..$19.95

The Best Country Songs Ever
Over 65 songs, featuring: Always on My Mind • Crazy • Daddy Sang Bass • Forever and Ever, Amen • God Bless the U.S.A. • I Fall to Pieces • Stand By Your Man • Through the Years • and more.
00359135..$16.95

The Best Easy Listening Songs Ever
A collection of 75 mellow favorites, featuring: All Out of Love • (They Long to Be) Close to You • Every Breath You Take • Eye in the Sky • How Am I Supposed to Live Without You • Imagine • Love Takes Time • Unchained Melody • Vision of Love • Your Song.
00359193..$18.95

The Best Gospel Songs Ever
80 of the best-loved gospel songs of all time: Amazing Grace • Daddy Sang Bass • His Eye Is on the Sparrow • How Great Thou Art • I'll Fly Away • Just a Closer Walk with Thee • Just a Little Talk with Jesus • The Old Rugged Cross • Will the Circle Be Unbroken • more.
00310503..$19.95

The Best Jazz Standards Ever
77 of the greatest jazz hits of all time, including: April in Paris • Body and Soul • Don't Get Around Much Anymore • Love Is Here to Stay • Misty • Out of Nowhere • Satin Doll • Unforgettable • When I Fall in Love • and many more.
00311641..$17.95

The Best Latin Songs Ever
67 songs, including: Adios • Besame Mucho (Kiss Me Much) • Blame It on the Bossa Nova • The Girl from Ipanema • Green Eyes • How Insensitive (Insensatez) • Malaguena • One Not Samba • Slightly Out of Tune (Desafinado) • Summer Samba (So Nice) • and more.
00310355..$17.95

The Best Love Songs Ever
A collection of 66 favorite love songs, including: (They Long to Be) Close to You • Endless Love • Here and Now • Longer • Love Takes Time • Misty • My Funny Valentine • So in Love • You Needed Me • Your Song.
00359198..$17.95

The Best Movie Songs Ever – 2nd Edition
This newly revised edition includes 74 songs made famous on the silver screen: Almost Paradise • Chariots of Fire • Circle of Life • I Will Wait for You • My Heart Will Go On • Take My Breath Away • Unchained Melody • You'll Be in My Heart • more.
00310063..$19.95

The Best R&B Songs Ever
66 songs, including: After the Love Has Gone • Baby Love • Dancing in the Street • Endless Love • Here and Now • I Will Survive • Saving All My Love for You • Stand By Me • What's Going On • and more.
00310184..$19.95

The Best Rock Songs Ever
70 songs, including: All Shook Up • Ballroom Blitz • Bennie and The Jets • Blue Suede Shoes • Born to Be Wild • Boys Are Back in Town • Every Breath You Take • Faith • Free Bird • Hey Jude • Louie, Louie • Maggie May • Money • We Got the Beat • Wild Thing • more!
00490424..$17.95

The Best Songs Ever
Over 70 must-own classics, including: All I Ask of You • Body and Soul • Crazy • Edelweiss • Love Me Tender • Memory • Moonlight in Vermont • My Funny Valentine • People • Satin Doll • Save the Best for Last • Strangers in the Night • Tears in Heaven • Unforgettable • The Way We Were • A Whole New World • and more.
00359224..$19.95

More of the Best Songs Ever
79 more favorites, including: Alfie • April in Paris • Autumn in New York • Beauty and the Beast • Beyond the Sea • Candle in the Wind • Don't Get Around Much Anymore • Endless Love • Falling in Love with Love • The First Time Ever I Saw Your Face • I've Got the World on a String • I've Grown Accustomed to Her Face • Misty • My Blue Heaven • My Heart Will Go On • Stella by Starlight • Witchcraft • more.
00310437..$19.95

The Best Standards Ever
Volume 1 (A-L)
72 beautiful ballads, including: All the Things You Are • Bewitched • Getting to Know You • God Bless' the Child • Hello, Young Lovers • It's Only a Paper Moon • I've Got You Under My Skin • The Lady Is a Tramp • Little White Lies.
00359231..$15.95

Volume 2 (M-Z)
72 songs, including: Makin' Whoopee • Misty • Moonlight in Vermont • My Funny Valentine • Old Devil Moon • The Party's Over • People Will Say We're in Love • Smoke Gets in Your Eyes • Strangers in the Night • Tuxedo Junction • Yesterday.
00359232..$15.95

FOR MORE INFORMATION, SEE YOUR LOCAL MUSIC DEALER, OR WRITE TO:

HAL•LEONARD™ CORPORATION
7777 W. BLUEMOUND RD. P.O. BOX 13819 MILWAUKEE, WI 53213

www.halleonard.com

Prices, contents and availability subject to change without notice. Not all products available outside the U.S.A.

0800